If only we realized that LOVE
is where His golden light enters…

GODZILLION WORLDS

A poetic collection of universes that exist beyond us

Lorenza Palomino

An Ink Gladiators Press® Publication

Ink Gladiators Press®
Publishing and promoting warriors on life's battlefield

Ink Gladiators Press is an ePublishing company whose mission is to publish and promote writers, poets, lyricists, artists and photographers through our current worldwide market distribution of over 3 billion readership. It is not affiliated with any other organization and is an independent ePublishing house. For Earthians who want to publish with us, check out our ongoing publishing opportunities at Our Earthians Community Group, or write to us to learn more about our high-end professional Celestial Sky Services at the following email address: contact@inkgladiatorspress.com.

First Edition

Godzillion Worlds

ISBN: 978-81-949418-7-3

Ink Gladiators Press®
Bangalore 560077, India
www.inkgladiatorspress.com

Credits:
Cover Photography & Photographs: Lorenza Palomino
Cover & Book Design - Leonie Belle Hawk
Editor-in-Chief - Reena Doss

This Chapbook is dedicated
to the universe of readers who will read this book.
I hope that it will encourage you in your daily life.

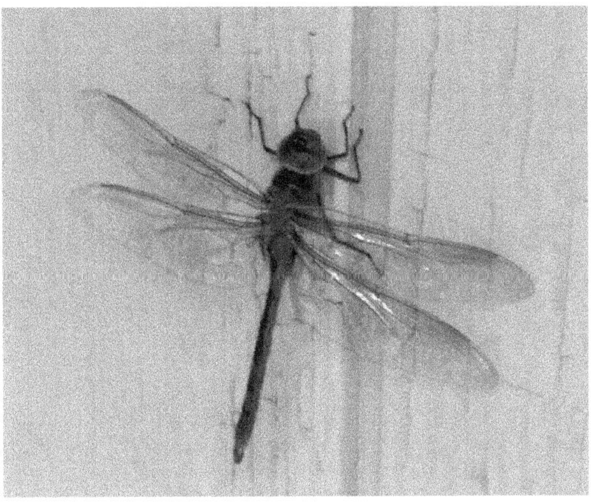

Table Of Contents

Author's Note

Dear brothers and sisters in Christ,

When I began writing about other worlds in the year 2008, my ultimate hope has always been to help others rise from the dreary dreams inside their minds and into the beautification of realism within; in order for all of us to reach our highest potential of true happiness and freedom. My burning passion for photography started in 2014 and which only enhanced my gift of writing and spreading the message of love even more.

Thanks for picking up Godzillion Worlds. I pray for love and light of the Holy Spirit to be with you always.

Grandeur Blessings!

@godzillionloveandlight
Instagram | Goodreads | Amazon
Email: dancingonglisteningwaters@gmail.com

Scan this QR code to follow Lorenza Palomino on Instagram.

Tell Us What You Think

Write to us at contact@inkgladiatorspress.com. We might add your comments or reviews on our website as well as feature your Instagram profile. We appreciate your love for reading. Thank you!

We remain at your service,
Reena Doss | Founder
Ink Gladiators Press®
www.inkgladiatorspress.com

Unfolding Worlds

I hand you a lily, invite you to get brainy.
No need to get hasty, for it is very easy.
It is the ability in every mind
to no longer be blind.

Everything that unfolds in worlds of illusion have all been prewritten before time was ignited. Scientists who study the universe do so through their own prewritten life script. I wish more scientists—who study the universe through spiritual vision—would come forward so we know they exist.

Everything we've always known is all bundled up inside, seeping through our dreams each time we go to sleep. We are co-authors but we are also co-creators and co-makers. This is one of the reasons why we also cohabit. Wouldn't it be nice if we spiritually synchronized ourselves to reach a peaceful and harmonious demise? Scientists who study the universe and who make it their life mission to know this through illusional physics have an enormous advantage over us to do this through spiritual vision. For to look at everything they have studied in the illusional context will all come together in an instant when viewed through God's eyes. This is true for each and every one of us. When we ask the Holy Spirit, He will take us on a divine ride through quantum leap and show us all we wish to know.

As it all comes together in a heartbeat through every mind's ability, there is an overwhelming eagerness to share this divine knowledge with the rest of the world. This generosity of mind is where we will find the glistening golden circle inside. But first, we must be willing to be open to this so it can take root and flourish to reveal the true geniuses that we are inside.

Rude Awakening

Born into a merciless world
destined to worship a premade ruthless father;
it sustains itself in us
where the mind and heart abide.

With every stride taken,
we are blind inside
to the divine fact instilled.
We can only behold and know this
through our willingness to rise
from the ego's cruel world
of fear and darkness.

We trespass ever so ruthlessly
because we think we are deserving of it
but this in itself is self-deceiving,
for all we are doing is conserving
the merciless temptation of sick thinking
into isolation and desolation.
We are callously selfish and greedy,
we do not care about the survival
of all those who are selfless and needy
like how we peel open layers of an onion
tearing our way to its core
to get to the juicy part of its tasty savories.

The journey of divinity
is a quantum leap
out of the fog of its clogged
and bleak thinking
where you find yourself sinking into
the abyss of its madness.

Don't you agree that it is the same journey
as we go through merciless temptation
to finally reach divine attraction into unity?

Courageous Gifts

Worlds of illusion bring about
devastations of fearful confusions.

Deep in our mind and heart,
we know that illusion is
senseless and meaningless
because it offers sufferings
mixed in with pleasures
for even those who bring
pain and suffering
upon others' do not like to suffer.

When the tables are turned,
they plea for us to stop
and let them live just as we did.
Yet it does not matter
who brings about pain and suffering,
because we all do it,
regardless of the form it rises in.
Under the divine power of courage
enters the spirit of kindness and humility
outshining the darkness within
and this is how everyone lives.

Let God remove the blindfold,
release the stronghold
and be blessed godzillion fold.
Have courage, be bold and fear not
for this enables you to behold
the essence of faith and hope.
The essence of courage
is kindness, humbleness and patience;
the center of love, joy and peace—
gifts planted inside
godzillions ago at the core of
mind, heart and soul.

For don't we all know,
that pleasures outrank sufferings?

The Separation

The excitement of the unknown
must have been ever so overwhelming.

But there comes a time when we behold
the significance of separation
and restoration into unification.
Separation is what caused
birth into illusional worlds
to dwell where we thought
it would be fine, dandy and swell
but the separation began in the desperation
to know what existed in the absence of love.

Would we find a world
caught in the savage of depression
deep in the agonies of troubles?
We coveted a force we had to make
and called it fear
knowing it would turn out
not to be so dear.
We forgot that love is what we are
and love is what we want.

Therefore, love is where we will return
under the wings of God's embrace.
It is only in worlds of fear
that we will find ourselves in tears.

O how could we have ever wanted to live
in a kingdom that would inevitably be undesirable?

Perfectly Braided

Everything we clash into brings
trauma, pain and sorrow
but this is exactly what dream worlds offer.

Through spiritual vision,
we behold and know in all clarity
the truth from the false in every aspect of life
on Earth,
the Universe
and Heaven.

Earth shaking, mountains exploding,
buildings crumbling, cars crashing, streets collapsing,
dirt sinking, mud sliding, ice melting, seas flooding,
heat overwhelming and everyone yelling.
Universe upholding hellish worlds,
burning stars, moons of calamity,
pulsating star lights, darkened moonlights,
galaxies galore and so much more.

In Heaven, everything is completely wide open
and nothing ever runs into each other.
Even if it did, everything will zoom
right through each other, tenderly embracing
one another in a dance of love.
There are no such things as explosions,
crumbling, clashing and collapsing.
Everything is perfect, for there are
no such things as accidents, trauma,
tears of fear and pains of sorrow.
This is because the glistening golden white vine
is forever divinely intertwined.

Everything in Heaven is perfectly braided
so that nothing ever falls apart.

Everyone and Everything

Through distorted thinking, we fear and hate
everyone and everything different from us.

In dreams, we pass judgment
upon everyone and everything,
for everyone and everything
we fear, hate, dislike,
complain about or even make fun of
are what we ourselves become.
In illusion, everyone and everything
are designs to act out what we are not.
To exhaust our thoughts
in the dreary fearsome circle
housing fear and hate
causes one to feel faint.

It is always pleasing to consume
our thoughts with the glory of light,
for it is here when we learn to love
everyone and everything
we fear, hate dislike,
complain about and make fun of.

To lay all negative forces
at God's golden feet
is to enable our eyes to be witnesses
to the transformation
from corruption to honesty.

The true reality is inside everyone and everything,
because Love is where the light enters...

The Only Law There Is

The laws of man will cease,
but the laws of God are the only laws
that will exist, eternally incorruptible.

Live comfortably in this world of illusional dreams,
but maintain righteousness in all your ways.
Just because someone points the finger
and accuses another does not make it so.
How easily we believe what others say
because we do not keep our own sick thinking at bay!

To keep our minds healthy
is to be willing to listen
to the soft, peaceful voice inside
to bind our virtuous ways
to God's meaningful laws
of forgiveness and redemption.

Meaningless laws are crazy ideas,
a harsh reality of a sick mentality
that will not last forever.
The meaningful laws of God
frees and enables us to spree in love forever.

It is possible to do this in a world of sickness
but all of us must be willing to listen
to the voice of thy Holy Spirit's guidance
who never brings about frightening things.
If He does, it is brief
with the comfort and peace of Christ
that always swiftly follows.

The only law that there is
are the laws of God's Love
that lead us to love, light, life and truth,
which is our royal inheritance.

Our Home

We think that the worst
that can happen is death.

Death is a transformation and transition
from a kingdom of corruption
to the Kingdom of beautification.
Yet, there is nothing
more beautiful than the liberty
of mortality to immortality,
particularly, when we transition
into the beauty of the Kingdom of Heaven
we have been gone from
since godzillions ago.

Transformation is a quantum leap process.
It is a transformation from mortality to immortality
where the spirit is released
from the imprisonment of the body.
It is where it transitions into eternal bliss.
In worlds of illusion, the worst that can happen
is to fight what is already inevitable.
This is where we prolong our suffering
and the best that can happen is
learning to surrender to the Holy Spirit
and let oneself go when the time arrives
for us to go home.
We prolong this because we do not remember
the eternal beauty of the Kingdom
we so long to be a part of.

Why stay in a Kingdom we do not belong
when God is calling us back home?

The Universe Within

We travel zillions of light years away
from our own Milky Way.

We still have not reached
the glorious natural light
of the glistening golden world of Heaven.
We started the galactic travels,
fresh, eager and hopeful
but find that we are worn, subdued
and hopeless by the voyage undertaken.
We started fresh zillions of light years ago
seeking Heaven outward
until we finally come to our divine senses
to search inward.

There is a universe within
where we find Heaven
because we are the love and light
of the glistening golden Heavenly Kingdom
that is vibrantly alive and well
thriving in abundant authentic life.
Godzillions ago,
we kept ourselves imprisoned in the darkness
where we remain blind to the light inside
where we behold everything.

Their life span and our own
has come to its end godzillion times over,
only to be replenished and rebirthed into it
again and again to occupy and become a slave
to the wrathful god we made.

The light of Heaven outshines the darkness,
for through spiritual vision
we behold that Heaven is inside us.

Worlds within a World

We spend a lifetime trying to figure out
what the universe is all about.

Great minds who study it
come up with theories of what it is
because they have not learned to remember
how to see it through spiritual vision and knowledge.
The universe is not a rock, moon or a star—
it is a world
and everything we behold in it
are worlds within a world.

Earth is a world and it is suspended
in the world of the universe
that houses all the other worlds
and everything else in it.
Heaven is a not a place, it is a Kingdom,
but it is the one true world
we will never find
in the vastness of the universe.
The universe is a world
where we witness all the other worlds within it
as far as our eyes, probes and telescopes can see
along with everything else we propped into it.

Everyone has a choice
as to which road they will take
to spiritually awake.

But through the eyes of God,
we can see beyond illusion to spiritual vision.

Born in the Land of Earth

We are born to be happy in the land of Earth
until we experience those dreadful feats.

We label each other
in an attempt to give names
to the mental and emotional issues
we wrestle with daily.
We are given pills
in an attempt to control the behaviors
that mental sicknesses dictate,
but medications are a temporary fix
that inevitably cause more
in-depth symptoms and adverse reactions
to the situations
we so desperately want to escape.

We are born in the land of earth
as experiencers to encounter
bittersweet combats in the battlefield of dreams,
which are merely lessons to learn by.
The moment we are born
out of timelessness into time,
the memory of all this is wiped out.
This is why we ask
the fundamental questions of blindness;
why, what, where, when, how
and if we are alone.

We are not alone, yet we ask the very minds
that do not know the answers.
Pills do not deliver us
from the mental states we spiral into
because it traps us in its circle of gloom,
but we are not forever doomed.
We may seem to be eternally lost,
but we can still be found.

Our state of minds can be restored
to who we truly are.

Black Hole

A recycle machine is powerful in its suction;
a force of its own source,
yet it would not be in existence
without everything else the universe upholds,
including us.

Black holes are powerful recycle machines, yet they are not clunks of metal that rust and settle. It does not run on fuel but sustains itself through its own duel of sovereignty which eventually turns on itself, just like everything else in dream worlds. However, before its lifespan runs out, the power in its recycle phase is immense as it has the ability to clean up all universal debris during its recycle spree. This has always been since time began.

They are merciless forces but they are also merciful points of sources because their suctions are so powerful. There comes a time when they also reverse their forces and something extraordinary and majestic happens in those moments, for they recycle everything to be renewed again, only to restart the illusional life cycle all over again. It can be termed as a tuning of communication if we just learn to remember how to master telepathic communication through divine meditation because we are transmitters no matter the distances between all forms of existence.

But, when will it all end?

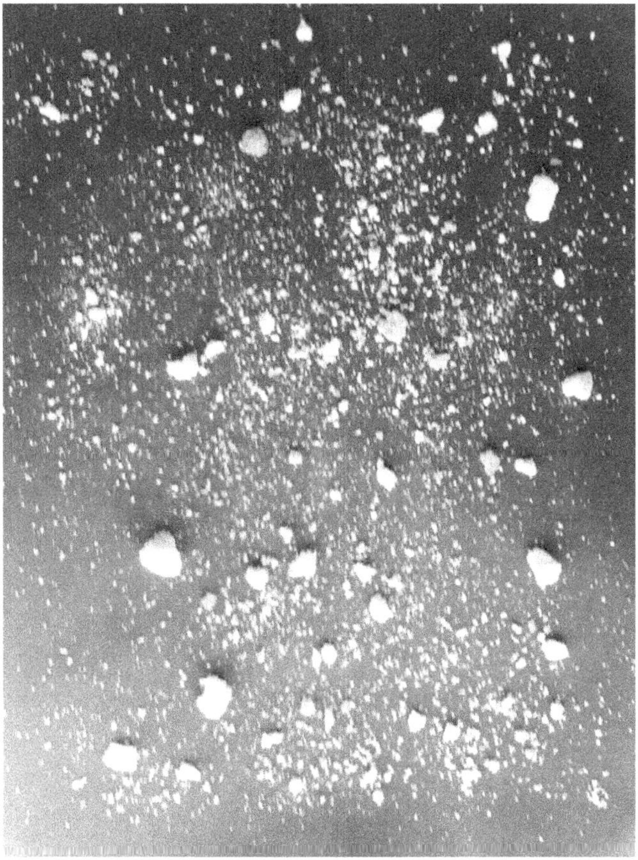

Our Story

Before we were born,
we wrote our deepest, darkest thoughts
of events that we would experience.

We wrote we would speak
of our most unthinkable experiences
of sufferings telling on one another.

Yet at the end of time,
none of it will even matter
because when we return to the holiness
of love and light, it supersedes
all the fear and darkness we encounter,
for in the presence of God's love,
nothing else matters.

His light outshines all ruthless misfortunes
on worlds of gloominess.
This is the true reality of an untainted Kingdom,
we have awaited godzillion years to return to.

The agreement we entered into before time,
makes my story yours
and your story mine
no matter the beauty
or how gory the details.

When I tell on you,
I am telling on myself
and when you tell on me,
you are telling on yourself.

Are we ready to be willingly delightful
as we reacquaint with who we truly are
and where we truly come from?

Sphere of God's Golden Light

Let us flourish
under the crown of the divine.

Expanding, I shall dance with them
in twirls and swirls,
intertwining in the sphere
of God's golden white vine
ever so pure and bright.
I gaze upon its vibrant light
outshining all fright, fight and flight.
I embrace its magnificence,
I know this is what is most significant.
Through the eyes of holiness,
it all makes sense.
As I relax without stress,
I feel at home in its presence
knowing it is such a blessing.
No reason to roll the dice
to the genesis of how
I came to pay the price.
Feeling tired and worn down,
I will accept the crown
of knowledge and understanding.
It's time to end the bloody,
get rid of all the money—
'tis the root of all evil.
It is possible to behold the sphere
of God's golden light within
if we are willing to look.

Let us embrace
the sphere of God's golden light.

Loving Surrender

Once I cross the threshold,
I hear the music no more.

We approach
the threshold of the open door
where I stand and bow my head
in humbleness and stillness.
With my feet planted,
I instinctively know in that moment,
my only desire is to remain there.
Listening to such glorious angelic hymns
brings me great contentment,
not wanting to go up yonder,
my feet remain planted as I ponder.

I step past the threshold,
I no longer hear the Heavenly music,
but I already knew I would not
once the door had closed.
I bow my head, asking,
"Am I dead?"

In this dimness,
I sense His essence of tranquility
and I am aware of His Majestic presence—
Pure white shining bright light
all around Him where He stands.
At the other end of the corridor,
with a welcoming smile
and wide open arms waiting,
ready to receive me.
I know I have always loved Him
and He has always loved me.
I vow I will never again
fall away from His love.

Since godzillions ago,
He has patiently awaited
and I softly surrender.

Walking With The Blind

Walking all over the earth
upside down and backward,
on a dream world full of actors.

We do spend a synthetic lifetime saying,
I want to follow my dreams.
I want my dream home.
I want a dream vacation
or *I want my dream car.*
In the world of dreams,
we follow man-made dreams
refusing to stop and think
how fake and worthless
all these things truly are.

All the things humanity needs to survive
are the only things that are useful,
like water, food, warmth and shelter
whereas most other things are useless
because we hardly ever use them,
like clothes and shoes in our closets.

As long as we elect to walk
upside down and backward,
we spiral downward.
All that we are
is meaningless and senseless
when we continue to be an actor.
Yet in learning how to walk forward and skyward,
we free ourselves from being blind actors
on a dream world full of nonsense.
It will release the binds, ties and straps
of handcuffs we have bond ourselves to.

What is the sense in paying for things
that wither, rust and turn to dust anyway?

Shattered Thoughts

O, why do my thoughts
bring on such fraught?

A battle of mixed emotions,
I want to drop my devotion.
I sometimes feel the goal of it shatters
like a tipped over glass top table
the forceful wind blew over
and glass explodes into millions of pieces.
I desperately wish to pick up
the fragments of the shattered glass
to place the bits and pieces back together again
to see the meaning behind the reasons
to my shattered thoughts.

I asked for a sign to tell me
if my shattered thoughts I must confine
or if your thoughts and mine are safe to share
when I clearly see many are not ready to care.

O Father, through discernment,
I behold the shattered glass as symbolic
to the vision of my shattered thoughts.
As I watch the battered world divide,
I pray for their willingness to unite.
The ego is the destroyer,
that always seeks to demolish.
I learn to discern to know
to disown its merciless thought pattern
to enable myself to stay
in God's love, light, faith and miracles.

Is this a sign of the unkindness of the ego
or the feeling of uncertainty
through my journey to certainty?

The Root of All Evil

True freedom lets us spree away
from the conflict of temptation.

We love to spend money.
We love to plan a bank heist.
We love to covet what others have.
We love to break into homes
to steal another's treasures in the hopes
that we will find a whole lot of loot.
We love to rob establishments at gun point
and demand their valuables and money.

Money and valuables
might be the initial temptation
toward harboring the love of money.
But it could also be
the feel of the thrill of spending money,
or maybe it is the adventure of the crime
of just stealing, killing or hurting.
But do we really love doing
what causes weariness and stress?
Is it really treasures we are after
or is it the adrenaline of the thrill we seek after?

Do we know why we choose to fall
into the temptation to steal, kill or destroy
when all it does is bring nervousness,
high anxiety and high stressful levels to others?
No matter what form the emotion arises in,
temptation is in everyone and everything.
I believe it is temptation that is the root of all evil
with the instinct of choice that is also within.

Can we let God purify this attraction of temptation
within the mind and the heart?

War Zone of the Mind's Eye

The moment we are born,
we are on a leash.

I did not foresee getting burnt
from a world that came to be
through the agreement
of you and me.

Born into a war zone household
veils the eyes and mind from everything else
except what you are going through.
Darkness prevails all attempts to escape
that inevitably befalls for a time
until every situation enters its end.
It takes time to find the way
out of the thick cloud of murkiness.
The ego takes hold and leads the way first
or else we would not be here
to experience its tainted affray.
We are its pets on chained leashes
and we easily accept this and follow
its dreadful lead into pain and sorrow.
Until the day our eyes will behold
a bright light above the murky night;
where we will begin to channel
the miracle of the inevitable.
Through phases of this revelation,
we will have begun a new chapter
toward redemption.

I sigh deeply, hoping that all life
will inescapably be freed
to witness the devastations
throughout the universe.

Christ enters and unleashes
the chains and shackles.

The Shepherd Of Lost Souls

Lucifer decided to take a ruthless backseat
and we followed his heartless influence.

He was not alone in his decision
to permit the speck of darkness
to rise in his beautiful heart.
We believed his fantasy was greater
than the golden glistening stream flowing
from the throne of God.
We go roaming on synthetic worlds
full of groaning and moaning.
The evidence of our sinful plots
is that we think it is all real.
In moments of coping
with all we brought into synthetic existence,
we forget that we are the makers of it.
But God's authentic holy promise
is that He would never forsake
His little children
who are His royal kindred.
No matter how deep we fall into disbelief,
God honors His holy promise
to every fallen angel and saint
right up till the end
of each synthetic life on dream worlds,
for He forgave us before time began.
We too must honor our holy promise
to our Father in Heaven
and to one another.
In relishing in God's laws
of forgiveness and redemption,
we are able to see that
the glistening golden umbilical cord
will never be severed.

He is the shepherd that herds God's lost souls
back to the glistening golden road of Heaven.

Forever Found

O how I cry out to find my way,
but I am only dazed.

I asked to let me see the light of Christ,
but there was no answer
and my heart felt knifed.
I did escape the iron fist of my household
and as I entered the world on my own,
the dark shadow once again transpired.
The light I once saw above the gloom
became a speck of light that dispersed
into dimness and the feeling of doom
once again bloomed.
I found myself blinded standing
in the midst of darkness;
for the light to my freedom
did not last very long.
I was already burned out from the battles
and wars from the house I escaped from.
I had no clue I would be stepping into
a bigger house full of its own conflicts.
Everywhere I turned, everyone was dealing
with their own hostilities. I was disappointed
and spiraled deeper into sadness.
Deep down in my heart,
I knew it would be best to try again
to find the light and remain in its delight
by laying it all at God's golden feet
to finally receive His gift of peace.
The day arrived when the speck of light
penetrated the murkiness of its shadows
upon the crown of our heads.
Each time, fear and darkness creeps up
with its harshness, forgive it and release it.

This is where we are truly free.
This is where I was found.

Glistening Golden Circle

He is the purity of divinity,
glistening into everyone and everything.

He is your creator
who built all divine creations
around His love and light
no matter their form.
At our own willingness,
we left the glistening golden circle
and the Kingdom of timelessness!
When everyone and everything
are willing to reach it
by looking past flesh and bones,
we can behold its glistening golden circle.

Holiness, sinlessness, wholeness, wholesomeness,
kindness, humbleness, peacefulness, guiltlessness,
compassion, joy, freedom, unity, safety, generosity,
immortality and royalty are the divine qualities
of the glistening golden circle.

Remember the divinity inside
enables you to embrace and behold
all the divine qualities
this glistening golden circle offers
because God never takes away
what He has already given at creation.
For one day, it will enable you
to share God's word
of love, light, life and truth
to ensure that everyone and everything
are found and led to divinity.

Worlds of illusion are the dreary bubbles
of synthetic pleasures, fears and sorrows.

Child of Godzillion

Child of godzillion years old,
we are forever fresh, young and clean as God is
because His light never burns out
and neither does our own.

Earth is a controlled environment not for experiments, but for experiences we asked to live out. The body is a prison that houses the spirit while we experience the fears of darkness. The sun is only a small portion of God's light that suspends itself in the atmosphere of the universe, shining upon the Earth. It also acts as a reminder of God's love and open light within.

When we gaze upwards, we are a witness to the shining burning sphere of light that God lends to sustain temporal life. Be happy we are not forever hurdled out into complete darkness where worlds of devastation also exist as far as our telescopes can see; worlds that we ourselves made that will destroy us. In fact, just the dark gravity alone will strangle us to death.

We are children of godzillion years old who are immensely loved by God. We are ancient, but forever young and vibrant. We are gorgeous and flawless spirits that never age. Our hair is never out of place, we have impeccable skin and we never get sick because this is the very nature of the spirit—this essence of immortality. However, our light can grow dim when we separate from Him and this is what we did.

This is why we are out in the universe until we rediscover the holiness of love and light within, which is to recognize through the Holy Spirit that God is the source of it, the essence of sinlessness and we are divinely connected to Him because God is at the core of everyone and everything.

Acknowledgement

My deepest thankfulness to Reena Doss and her team at Ink Gladiators Press for their utmost professional support, creative ideas and suggestions. Their skills in formatting and forming this chapbook to its highest potential is beyond anything I could ever have imagined.

I am beyond excited as we are currently preparing the publication of my next book which is the first volume from a trilogy—Glistening Golden Circle. I am filled with gratitude towards their dedication in bringing my poetic spiritual visions to the world. It amazes me that Reena complements my mind. What I do not think of, she does and what she does not think of, I think of. It is exactly like majestic minds intertwined with lovely creativity.

There is no doubt in my mind that Reena and her team are a majestic blessing on a godzillion scale. Their creative support in getting Godzillion Worlds, my debut chapbook has been a majestic gift.

Thank you!

Grandeur Blessings,

www.ingramcontent.com/pod-product-compliance
Lightning Source LLC
Chambersburg PA
CBHW062204160726
48282CB00027B/984
* 9 7 8 8 1 9 4 9 4 1 8 7 3 *

If only we realized that LOVE
is where His golden light enters...